THE STRANGE ISLANDS

Also by Thomas Merton

THE ASCENT TO TRUTH

BREAD IN THE WILDERNESS

FIGURES FOR AN APOCALYPSE

THE LIVING BREAD

NO MAN IS AN ISLAND

SEEDS OF CONTEMPLATION

THE SEVEN STOREY MOUNTAIN

THE SIGN OF JONAS

THE TEARS OF THE BLIND LIONS

THE WATERS OF SILOE

THE

STRANGE

ISLANDS

POEMS BY THOMAS MERTON

A NEW DIRECTIONS BOOK

Design by Stefan Salter

Some of the poems in this volume have appeared in
the following magazines, to the editors of which grate-
ful acknowledgement is hereby given: *Commonweal,
Jubilee, New World Writing, Sign* and *Thought.*

New Directions Books are published at Norfolk, Conn.,
by James Laughlin. New York office—333 Sixth
Ave. (14)

Manufactured in the United States of America by
The Haddon Craftsmen, Scranton, Penna.

For Mark and Dorothy Van Doren

EX PARTE ORDINIS

CONTENTS

PREFACE

This book contains the work of seven or eight years—or rather work that was spread out over that period, though most of the poems actually belong to 1955 and 1956. "Sports Without Blood" was to have been included in an earlier volume (*Tears of the Blind Lions*) and has already been printed in the author's *Selected Poems* (London, 1952). The "Prelude for the Feast of St. Agnes appeared in *The Sign of Jonas*. Several of these poems were produced in response to a "billet" from the New York Carmel. Carmelites have to draw by lot a subject for a Christmas song which they compose and sing at the crib on the Feast of Our Lord's Nativity. "The Annunciation," "Stranger" and "Elias" are such poems, though "Elias" hardly turned out to be a carol or even a Christmas poem. It simply represents what the author had going through his head in the Christmas season of 1954.

The three parts into which the book is divided have nothing to do with chronological sequence. The more recent poems are scattered about in Parts One and Three—("Anatomy of Melancholy," "Exploits of a Machine Age," "Sincerity," "Birdcage Walk," "Nocturne," "Landscape," and "The Severe Nun," for instance). "Elegy for the Monastery Barn" was written after the cowbarn at Gethsemani burned down, one August evening in 1953, during the evening meditation. The monks left the meditation to fight a very hot fire and the poem arrived about the same time as the fire truck from the nearest town.

PART ONE

HOW TO ENTER A BIG CITY

I

Swing by starwhite bones and
Lights tick in the middle.
Blue and white steel
Black and white
People hurrying along the wall.
"Here you are, bury my dead bones."

Curve behind the sun again
Towers full of ice. Rich
Glass houses, "Here,
Have a little of my blood,
Rich people!"

Wheat in towers. Meat on ice.
Cattlecars. Miles of wide-open walls.
Baseball between these sudden tracks.
Yell past the red street—
Have you any water to drink, City?
Rich glass buildings, give us milk!
Give us coffee! Give us rum!

There are huge clouds all over the sky.
River smells of gasoline.
Cars after cars after cars, and then
A little yellow street goes by without a murmur.

There came a man
("Those are radios, that were his eyes")
Who offered to sell us his bones.

Swing by starwhite buildings and
Lights come to life with a sound
Of bugs under the dead rib.

Miles of it. Still the same city.

II

Do you know where you are going?
Do you know whom you must meet?

Fortune, perhaps, or good news
Or the doctor, or the ladies
In the long bookstore,
The angry man in the milkbar
The drunkard under the clock.
Fortune, perhaps, or wonder
Or, perhaps, death.

In any case, our tracks
Are aimed at a working horizon.
The buildings, turning twice about the sun,
Settle in their respective positions.
Centered in its own incurable discontent, the
    City
Consents to be recognized.

III

Then people come out into the light of afternoon,
Covered all over with black powder,
And begin to attack one another with statements
Or to ignore one another with horror.
Customs have not changed.
Young men full of coffee and
Old women with medicine under their skin
Are all approaching death at twenty miles an hour.

Everywhere there is optimism without love
And pessimism without understanding,
They who have new clothes, and smell of haircuts
Cannot agree to be at peace
With their own images, shadowing them in windows
From store to store.

IV

Until the lights come on with a swagger of frauds
And savage ferns,
The brown-eyed daughters of ravens,
Sing in the lucky doors
While night comes down the street like the millennium
Wrapping the houses in dark feathers
Soothing the town with a sign
Healing the strong wings of sunstroke.
Then the wind of an easy river wipes the flies
Off my Kentucky collarbone.

The claws of the treacherous stars
Renegade drums of wood
Endure the heavenward protest.
Their music heaves and hides.
Rain and foam and oil
Make sabbaths for our wounds.
(Come, come, let all come home!)

The summer sighs, and runs.
My broken bird is under the whole town,
My cross is for the gypsies I am leaving
And there are real fountains under the floor.

v

Branches baptize our faces with silver
Where the sweet silent avenue escapes into the hills.
Winds at last possess our empty country
There, there under the moon
In parabolas of milk and iron
The ghosts of historical men
(Figures of sorrow and dust)
Weep along the hills like turpentine.
And seas of flowering tobacco
Surround the drowning sons of Daniel Boone.

THE GUNS OF FORT KNOX

Guns at the camp (I hear them suddenly)
Guns make the little houses jump. I feel
Explosions in my feet, through boards.
Wars work under the floor. Wars
Dance in the foundations. Trees
Must also feel the guns they do not want
Even in their core.
As each charge bumps the shocked earth
They shudder from the root.

Shock the hills, you guns! They are
Not too firm even without dynamite.
These Chinese clayfoot hills
Founded in their own shale
Shift their feet in friable stone.

        Such ruins cannot
Keep the armies of the dead
From starting up again.
They'll hear these guns tonight
Tomorrow or some other time.
They'll wake. They'll rise
Through the stunned rocks, form
Regiments and do death's work once more.

Guns, I say, this is not
The right resurrection. All day long
You punch the doors of death to wake

A slain generation. Let them lie
Still. Let them sleep on,
O Guns. Shake no more
(But leave the locks secure)
Hell's door.

NOCTURNE

Night has a sea which quenches the machine
Or part of it. Night has tides of rain
And sources which go on
Washing our houses when we turn to dream.

Night has, for flesh and ghost, a weak-eyed sun
Whose light the anxious living fear. Shapes of the dead
Make legends with the rest of us: that all
Must miss some train, be late at school,
Found without money in the strange hotel.

O night, whose golden spark in the safe mind
Explores all countries where the soul has gone,
Explain the colored shapes whose hundreds
Fly in the wind from every broken pod.

O one-eyed night, whose wisdom sails from God
By deep canals to heave and change our falls,
Your choirs amaze the thoughtful heart.
What were the notes, then, of your sacred tone
Uttering, while thought was stopped,
The one prophetic question?

If I could answer you, your tides and histories
Would end, or would begin all storms.

SPRING STORM

When in their ignorance and haste the skies must fall
Upon our white-eyed home, and blindly turn
Feeling the four long limits of the wall,

How unsubstantial is our present state
In the clean blowing of those elements
Whose study is our problem and our fate?

The intellects go mumbling in the snow,
And find the blurred, incredible sun (and moon)
Jammed in the white door, and the troubled straits
The dugout where the fallen sky lies down.
A mess of secret trumpets, with their weight
Of portents, veil the bluntness where we run.

How true a passion has this hour begun!
The sky melts on my patient animal
(My pointless self, the hunter of my home),
My breath burns in the open like a ton
In the blue waking of those elements
Whose study is our quibble and our doom.

O watch the woolen hundreds on the run!

WHETHER THERE IS ENJOYMENT IN BITTERNESS

This afternoon, let me
Be a sad person. Am I not
Permitted (like other men)
To be sick of myself?

Am I not allowed to be hollow,
Or fall in the hole
Or break my bones (within me)
In the trap set by my own
Lie to myself? O my friend,
I too must sin and sin.

I too must hurt other people and
(Since I am no exception)
I must be hated by them.

Do not forbid me, therefore,
To taste the same bitter poison,
And drink the gall that love
(Love most of all) so easily becomes.

Do not forbid me (once again) to be
Angry, bitter, disillusioned,
Wishing I could die.

While life and death
Are killing one another in my flesh,
Leave me in peace. I can enjoy,
Even as other men, this agony.

Only (whoever you may be)
Pray for my soul. Speak my name
To Him, for in my bitterness
I hardly speak to Him: and He
While He is busy killing me
Refuses to listen.

SPORTS WITHOUT BLOOD — A LETTER TO DYLAN THOMAS (1948)

I

In old King George's June
When evening drowned and sang in the peeled water,
Hate took place in Cambridge, and a cricketer's death
Under the tents of Chesterton.

It was to be a night without religion.
The houses rumpled their ancient skins:
The century still thundered at their doors.
   "Now here they come, down the abiding sky
   Lovers of many monies under the sun.
   Crosscolored bodies, in which is vanity.
   Hush-hush waters cripple the world that's upside down,
   And lives are flights on the face of motherofpearl heaven
   Until old crossbones get their skulls in greysize capture.
   The race is over. Life and death are even."

In this same night of ales
I was uprooted by my own ghost
Not without fury and
Not without cost.
The rivers mummed, grandfathers
Grumbled at my door.
War in the water and war on the grass,
War in the belly and feet and face,
(Crosscolored bodies in which is vomiting)
The war in the river was, perhaps, worse:
The upside down were last and first.

"Thus did the oarsmen feel the waters of their fen
(With dog-drunk gasbodies winning under the tank)
Scattering the shadows of a railway bridge
And seven willow women mad as trees:
They smashed the gas river over and under,
The blue-brown river, bad as drink."
Their smiles have shivered all that order
And boats slide down their oil on an army of wrinkles
While blades replace the upside down cathedrals
With a wallop of bells.

In old King George's attic
When everything went black in the piled city
Pain took place in colleges, and bloodless sports
Under the tents of Chesterton.

II

Old Joe and Rosa's martyr
Seven principal oarsmen and Jack-John the lad of the lawns
Planted a relic of our spotting biograph
Here, in a spell between two bombs.
And here we bloom, amid the marigolds
Sad, with the central doll of an old photo,
The treeless grills, and the pelouse.

Oh, the bald lawns, and the enclosure
The green we had to smell!
What subtle matter for an effigy
Between the door and the wall:

And there the old, whose airless voice
Fell from our England's winding sheet,
Withdrew their leaves, let George and Dragon
Drown in the porter's little room.
All the bodies dangle in a garden of bowls.

But you proceeded to the burial.
Night by night in Camden Town
Up and down the furry buildings,
In and out the boxing alleys, dark as tea
You walked with murder in your music box
And played the pieces of blind England all around the down.

Thus the men lay down to sleep in the pavilion
With a whisper of flannel and leather;
The ladies all arranged themselves upon the ground
With a wuthering of old fowls:
And now from their ten million pots and pipes
Their dreams crept out and fumed at the wet night,
While they slept in the cloud without Christ.
Then angels ploughed them under the ground
With little songs as sharp as needles
And words that shone by night as bright as omens.

III

Blind northern friends, whose hopeless manor
Fox and grouse have come to own,
Bred hand in glove with pestilence
The ivy eats your castle down.

The horns of thunder drown and die
When evenings sing their frittered song.
The sonnets of my tearless eye
Shine on the city's second string.

Cling to the city's second rung
While oarsmen feel their frozen fen:
And boat by boat their tocsins ring
And house by house their walls cave in.

Then the blue pleasures are destroyed
Whose seas concern the oarsman's blade.
The halls are severed, bridges bleed
And the drowned world is animate,

Till the brown boats, devouring all,
Wipe out the city's second spring,
Sail on, while the cathedrals fall
And feel what rain the bellnotes bring.

Before the formal racers come
And puzzles are once more unfurled,
Come, let us drink our poisoned home
And swim in the face of a glass world!

All the world's waters whimper and cry
And evils eat body and soul.
The times have carried love away.
And tides have swallowed charity.

Bound, bound, my fens, whose soundless song
Both verse and prose have come to end.
It is the everlasting wrong:
Our cities vanish in the wind.

IV

They have given the cricketer a grass heart
And a dry purse like a leaf, Look!
Look! The little butterflies come out!
He was wounded, he was wounded in the wars
Where the roots our umpires are.
It is a funny death, when flowers undermine castles.
O Listen to their calls
Listen to their wooden calls.
"Chop-chop," says bats (or blocks):
But we shall drive in another direction,
Leaving this people to its own calm,
And turn again to waters brown, whose underlights,
Whose manners are insane
With the oars of the young man trained
To separate a mirror into riddles.

Come, let us die in some other direction
Sooner than the houses in the river quiver and
    begin their dance
And fall in the terrible frown.

EXPLOITS OF A MACHINE AGE

For Robert Lax

Once again they were dismayed
By their own thin faces in the morning. They

Hoped they would not die today either.
They hoped for some light
Breakfast and a steady hand.

To the protected work
They fled, to the unsafe machinery
They lived by. "It will go better this time.
We have arranged, at last,
To succeed. Better luck
This time."

So they went to the
Guarded plant, muttering, "Better luck,
Better luck,"
(Till the clowns in the sun cried,
"Then He struck!").

But no! Nothing was felt or heard.
Once again the explosion was
Purely mental. It shook them, though,
And they went pale around noon.
The machines were safe. Nothing
At all had happened.
Literally nothing.

Exhausted by this nothing, they
Came home, faced the steadfast apartment,
Globes, windows, and even moon.
And they made up their minds.

They climbed into their dwellings, grim
As yesterday, and always muttering,
"Better luck tomorrow!"

THE ANATOMY OF MELANCHOLY

There was a man, born like
Other men, but he had a
Different name. He always

Took himself seriously
And kept his head before it was too late,
Because his nurse had
Struck him in the cradle.

Wherever he went he kept his
Eye on the clock. His heart was not
On his sleeve, but his tongue was ready
With a civil answer.

One day he could not find his feet.
He lost his balance and began to sing:
When he sang, they paid him to shut up,
He was no longer happy when he smiled.

He tried to walk and they
Put him in jail. He spoke
And showed a broken tooth.
When he sat down he lost face.

It was a long night before he woke up
And was found beside himself when he
Came to his senses.
No one cared to have him around

Though his heart was in the right place
Clucking like a hen.

No one remembered but the business men
Who entered brandishing a bill.
They greeted him and smiled as they sat.
"You have," they said (as he lost his voice)
"A serious problem."
So they took away his house.
The cops went off
With his sister and daughter.
He kept a stiff upper lip but no
Money and no social standing.

"What shall I do?" he cried, "drink or gamble?"
He left in no direction, followed by his dog
(The dog is man's best friend), and

Puritans had them arrested
For romping as they walked
And barking as they spoke.

ELIAS — VARIATIONS ON A THEME

I

Under the blunt pine
In the winter sun
The pathway dies
And the wilds begin.
Here the bird abides
Where the ground is warm
And sings alone.

Listen, Elias,
To the southern wind
Where the grass is brown,
Live beneath this pine
In wind and rain.
Listen to the woods,
Listen to the ground.

O listen, Elias
(Where the bird abides
And sings alone),
The sun grows pale
Where passes One
Who bends no blade, no fern.
Listen to His word.

"Where the fields end
Thou shalt be My friend.

Where the bird is gone
Thou shalt be My son."

How the pine burns
In the furious sun
When the prophets come
To Jerusalem.
(Listen, Elias,
For the fiery wing)
To Jerusalem
Where the knife is drawn.
(Do her children run
To the covering wing?
Look, look, My son,
At the smashed wood
At the bloody stone.

Where the fields end
And the stars begin
Listen, Elias,
To the winter rain.
For the seed sleeps
By the sleeping stone.
But the seed has life
While the stone has none.

"Where the fields end
Thou shalt be My friend.
Where the bird is gone
Thou shalt be My son."

There were supposed to be
Not birds but spirits of flame
Around the old wagon.
("Bring me my chariot")
There were supposed
To be fiery devices,
Grand machines, all flame,
With supernatural wings
Beyond the full creek.
("Bring me my chariot of fire")
All flame, beyond the rotten tree!
Flame? This old wagon
With the wet, smashed wheels
Is better. ("My chariot")
This derelict is better.
("Of fire.") It abides
(Swifter) in the brown ferns
And burns nothing. Bring me ("Of fire")
Better still the old trailer ("My chariot")
With the dead stove in it, and the rain
Comes down the pipe and covers the floor.
Bring me my chariot of rain. Bring me
My old chariot of broken-down rain.
Bring, bring my old fire, my old storm,
My old trailer; faster and faster it stands still,
Faster and faster it stays where it has always been,
Behind the felled oaks, faster, burning nothing.
Broken and perfect, facing south,

Facing the sound of distant guns,
Facing the wall of distance where blue hills
Hide in the fading rain.

Where the woods are cut down the punished
Trailer stands alone and becomes
(Against all the better intentions of the owners)
The House of God
The Gate of Heaven.
("My chariot of fire")

III

The seed, as I have said,
Hides in the frozen sod.
Stones, shaped by rivers they will
Never care about or feel,
Cover the cultivated soil.

The seed, by nature, waits to grow and bear
Fruit. Therefore it is not alone
As stones, or inanimate things are:
That is to say, alone by nature,
Or alone forever.

Where do so many waters come from on an empty hill?
Rain we had despaired of, rain
Which is sent from somewhere else, descended
To fix an exhausted mountain.
Listen to the waters, if possible,

And discern the words "False prophet"
False prophet! "So much better is the water's message,
So much more confident than our own. It is quite sure
You are a false prophet, so 'Go back'
(You have not had the patience of a rock or tree)
Go back into the cities. They want to receive you
Because you are not sent to them. You are a false prophet."

Go back where everyone, in heavy hours,
Is of a different mind, and each is his own burden,
And each mind is its own division
With sickness for diversion and war for
Business reasons. Go where the divided
Cannot stand to be too well. For then they would be held
Responsible for their own misery.

And I have been a man without silence,
A man without patience, with too many
Questions. I have blamed God
Thinking to blame only men
And defend Him Who does not need to be defended.
I have blamed ("defended") Him for Whom the wise stones
(Stones I lately condemned)
Waited in the patient
Creek that is now wet and clean of all ruins.

So now, if I were to return
To my own city (yes my own city), I would be
Neither accepted nor rejected.
For I have no message,
I would be lost together with the others.

Under the blunt pine
I who am not sent
Remain. The pathway dies,
The journey has begun.
Here the bird abides
And sings on top of the forgotten
Storm. The ground is warm.
He sings no particular message.
His hymn has one pattern, no more planned,
No less perfectly planned
And no more arbitrary
Than the pattern in the seed, the salt,
The snow, the cell, the drop of rain.

   (Snow says: I have my own pattern;
   Rain says: no arbitrary plan!
   River says: I go my own way.
   Bird says: I am the same.
   The pine tree says also:
   Not compulsion plants me in my place,
   No, not compulsion!)

The free man is not alone as busy men are
But as birds are. The free man sings
Alone as universes do. Built
Upon his own inscrutable pattern
Clear, unmistakable, not invented by himself alone
Or for himself, but for the universe also.

Nor does he make it his business to be recognized
Or care to have himself found out
As if some special subterfuge were needed
To get himself known for who he is.

The free man does not float
On the tides of his own expedition
Nor is he sent on ventures as busy men are,
Bound to an inexorable result:
But like the birds or lilies
He seeks first the Kingdom, without care.
Nor need the free man remember
Any street or city, or keep campaigns
In his head, or countries for that matter
Or any other economy.

                    Under the blunt pine
Elias becomes his own geography
(Supposing geography to be necessary at all),
Elias becomes his own wild bird, with God in the center,
His own wide field which nobody owns,
His own pattern, surrounding the Spirit
By which he is himself surrounded:

For the free man's road has neither beginning nor end.

PART TWO

THE TOWER OF BABEL

A Morality

The whole earth used the same language and the same speech. While men were migrating eastward, they discovered a valley in the land of Sennaar and settled there. They said to one another, "Come, let us make bricks and bake them." They used bricks for stone and bitumen for mortar. Then they said, "Let us build ourselves a city and a tower with its top in the heavens; let us make a name for ourselves lest we be scattered all over the earth." The LORD *came down to see the city and the tower which men had built. And the* LORD *said, "Truly they are one people and they all have the same language. This is the beginning of what they will do. Let us go down, and there confuse their language so that they will not understand one another's speech." So the* LORD *scattered them from that place all over the earth; and they stopped building the city. For this reason it was called Babel, because there the* LORD *confused the speech of all the earth.*—GENESIS 11:1-9.

*Two kinds of love have created two Cities: the earthly city
is created by the love of self to the point of contempt for
GOD: the heavenly city by love of GOD to the point of self-
contempt. The earthly city glories in herself only, the
heavenly glories in the LORD. The earthly city seeks her
glory from men, the heavenly, through the witness of a good
conscience, finds GOD in herself as her supreme glory. The
earthly city loves her own power, but the heavenly turns to GOD
and says "I will love Thee, o GOD my strength!" . . .*

—St. Augustine, THE CITY OF GOD, xiv, 28.

*And a mighty angel took up a stone, as it were a great
millstone and cast it into the sea saying: with such violence as
this shall Babylon that great city be thrown down and shall
be found no more at all. . . . For all nations have been deceived by
her enchantments, and in her was found the blood of prophets and
of saints and of all that were slain upon the earth.*

APOCALYPSE 18: 21,23-24.

PART ONE—The Legend of the Tower
Scene One—The Building of the Tower

RAPHAEL, THOMAS, FIRST BUILDER, SECOND BUILDER, LEADER, CAPTAIN, CHORUS

[*Musical Prelude—the building of the Tower. Enter* RAPHAEL *and* THOMAS.

THOMAS:	Ought we, Raphael, to join
	The builders of this city?
	We can quickly learn
	Their language and their ambition.
RAPHAEL:	No, we must stand apart.
	If we learn their language
	We will no longer understand
	What is being said.
	If we imitate their zeal
	We will lose all sense of what is to be done.
THOMAS:	They are clear-minded men
	Of one purpose.
RAPHAEL:	No. They only appear
	To know what they are building.
	They think it is a tower
	That will reach heaven.
	They think they speak the same
	Language, that they are of one
	Mind.
	Presently
	We shall discover that they are

Only of one voice. Many minds,
Many thoughts signifying nothing.
Many words, many plans
Without purpose. Divided hearts,
Weak hands. Hearts that will be
Closed to one another. Hands
Armed against one another.
There is no agreement
There can be no tower.

FIRST BUILDER: I believe in the tower.
Therefore I will work longer hours.

SECOND BUILDER: I believe in the Leader.
Therefore I will sacrifice myself
To build this tower.

FIRST BUILDER: I believe in our common language,
Therefore I will serve the Leader.

SECOND BUILDER: I believe in labor without reward.
The Tower is reward enough.

FIRST BUILDER: I believe in work without food and sleep
Although it is not yet possible.

SECOND BUILDER: The Leader will make it possible.

FIRST BUILDER: Everyone knows that the Leader
Will make everything possible.

SECOND BUILDER: It is good that we agree brother.
Let us never stop working;
Let us build this Tower for the Leader who loves war.

FIRST BUILDER: Yet, it is good that we agree. Let us
Build this Tower for the Leader who loves peace.

CAPTAIN: Silence! Stop work. Listen to the Leader.

LEADER: The Tower is nearly finished.

It is the greatest of all Towers, in fact
It is the only perfect and eternal Tower. There has
   never been
And never will be another such Tower.
The Tower is inviolable. It will
Be attacked by invisible powers
From above and from below by agents of social
   corruption.
Are you tired of work, my people?
Then, when the Tower is built,
We shall have war. But the Tower is impregnable.
Do your duty. Soon you will
Taste the excitement of war.

CAPTAIN: Back to work. The Tower must be finished by night-
   fall.

CHORUS: Grow Babylon, grow,
Great Babylon, touch the stars.
What if the Lord should see you, now?
Grow, Babylon, Grow!

RAPHAEL
[*The dialogue
continues
against the
background of
the* CHORUS]: They suppose that if they build a high tower very quickly, they will be nearly as strong as God, Whom they imagine to be only a little stronger than themselves. And if the highest part of the tower is level with the lowest part of heaven, man and God will have to discuss everything on equal terms.

THOMAS: It is therefore a religious tower, and they are men of faith.

RAPHAEL: No, it is a tower of unbelief.

THOMAS: What have they failed to believe in?

RAPHAEL: Two things: First they do not believe in themselves, and because of this they do not believe in God. Because they do not believe in themselves or in God, they cannot believe in unity. Consequently they cannot be united. Therefore they cannot finish the tower which they imagine they are building.

THOMAS: Nevertheless they are very busy with whatever they think they are doing.

RAPHAEL: That is a pretense. Activity is their substitute for faith. Instead of believing in themselves, they seek to convince themselves, by their activity, that they exist. And their activity pretends to direct itself against God, in order that they may reassure themselves that He does not exist.

THOMAS: Why so?

RAPHAEL: Because if He does not exist, then they do not have to be troubled with the problem of their own existence either. For if they admit they exist they will have to love one another, and this they find insupportable.

THOMAS: But surely they love one another! Otherwise how could they unite in a common endeavor? Surely, they are united, and their union has brought them success.

RAPHAEL: No, they have only united in their common, though hidden, desire to fail. Their ambition is only the occasion for a failure they certainly seek. But they require that this failure come upon them, as it were, out of the stars. They want to blame their ruin on fate, and still have the secret satisfaction of ruining themselves.

THOMAS: Why should they do so much work in order to fail?

RAPHAEL: Their hearts seek disaster as a relief from the tedium of an unsatisfactory existence. Ruin will at least divide them from one another. They will be able to scatter, to run away, to put barricades against one another. Since they cannot stand the pretense of unity, they must seek the open avowal of their enmity.

FIRST BUILDER: What is this thing called war which has been promised us as our reward for finishing the tower?

SECOND BUILDER: It is another work invented by the Leader, more glorious than this one as well as more exhausting.

CAPTAIN: Silence. Stop work! The Leader will ascend to the garden he has planted on the summit of the Tower he has built. He will walk and sing under the exotic trees upon whose branches he will presently hang the heads of our common enemies.

LEADER: Already I see that the skies are as full of words as they are of stars. Each word becomes an instrument of war. Words of the clocks and devils. Words of the wheels and machines. Steel words stronger than flesh or spirit. Secret words which divide the essences of things. Last of all, the one word which strikes at the heart of creation, and dissolves it into its original nothingness. Give me possession of this one word, and I will forget every other.

CHORUS: Fear! Fear!
Feel the business that springs
Out of the dark. Feel fear pass cold
hands (like wind) over your skin!
Fear talks out of the thundercloud.
Ships fold their wings. The almond trees
Grow pale before the storm.

[CHORUS *continues as background to following dialogue.*]

THOMAS: Raphael, I am scared, I see the tower nodding against the moon. I see the great cranes bending under the cloud.

RAPHAEL: Look at the little boats, Thomas, how they fly down the river. See how the carts topple off the side of the road!

THOMAS: O Raphael, that cloud first came up out of the desert no bigger than a man's fist. Then at once it stood over the tower like a man's arm. Then suddenly the burly dark filled the whole sky. Can you still hear me in this wind?

RAPHAEL: Wind with a thousand fingers pulls away the scaffolding. With a thousand invisible fists the wind beats on the battlements of the great Tower.

FIRST WATCHMAN: Blow the trumpets! Blow the storm-warning trumpet!

VOICE: It is too late, the storm is already upon us.

WATCHMAN: Blow the fire trumpet, blow the fire trumpet!

VOICE: It is too late. Fire has sprouted from a hole in the Tower!

CHORUS: Hide us from the fall, hide us from the fall!
Hide us in the catacomb, hide us in the well!
Hide us in the ground, hide us from the sky!
Hide us from the Tower's fall!

WATCHMAN: Blow the poison trumpet, blow the poison trumpet!

VOICE: Too late! The captains have already taken poison.

WATCHMAN: Then blow the trumpet of division.

VOICE: Blow the trumpet of division!

THOMAS: This is Babylon's end!

RAPHAEL: No, it is Babylon's beginning!

CHORUS: Now blow upon this plain you winds of heaven.
Blow, blow, you winds of God, upon the sands.
Scatter the seeds of war to the world's end.

Scene Two—The Trial

RAPHAEL, THOMAS, SOLDIERS, CAPTAIN, LEADER, PROFESSOR, PROPAGANDA, FALSEHOOD, LANGUAGE, CHORUS

[SCENE—*Square in a half-ruined city.* RAPHAEL *and* THOMAS.]

RAPHAEL: Everywhere the great machines of war
Stand face to face. The hunters in the sky
Bargain with life and death.
Babylon, like a great star wandering from its orbit,
Unsettles the universe, dragging nations down into
    chaos.

THOMAS: Is this the same city? All the cities in the world
Begin to look like the same city.
Wagons come down to the water
Where the crowds stand
After flags have fallen. Angry men
Stand without speech,
Wait for the conquering army.

SOLDIERS [*enter, singing marching song*]:
The bar snake and the zigzag snake
Will bite each other in the head
And drown each other in the river:
Who will reign when both are dead?
The fire bird and the water bird
Have brought good luck to Babylon
But who will reign when both are dead?

CAPTAIN: Gather the citizens in the square
And fill the whole city
With the sound of one voice.

There shall be no other voice. For peace,
Peace is this: only a giant voice.
There shall be one Babylon, fearing the orator.
There shall be one Babylon, hating itself.
[*Enter* LEADER, PROFESSOR, LAWYERS.]

LEADER: Now we must settle the question of guilt.
The Tower fell. Babylon was dishonored.
Our armies, though everywhere victorious,
Are full of traitors. Sabotage
Halts the production of new weapons.
Who is responsible?

CHORUS: Nothing is light, nothing is dark,
Nothing is defined. Sunlight and darkness
Both bring forth new fear.
Things are beginning to lose their names,
Persons their character. All
Wear the look of death, and become terrible.

CAPTAIN: Silence! Traitors. Salute the Leader!
He brings you life, salvation,
Prosperity, peace. Can you not see that despair,
Unhappiness, will presently cease to exist?

LEADER: Who has taught these people the lies they utter?
What enemy has poisoned their minds?

CAPTAIN: We know the traitor's name,
One who was at first our best friend, one who was
Our most capable officer. One we thought
Would not fail us.

LEADER: Who is it then?

CAPTAIN: Language! He and his regiments, the words,
Have sold out to the enemy.

LEADER: Impossible.
               Words have always been our best soldiers.
               They have defeated meaning in every engagement
               And have almost made an end of reality.

CAPTAIN: No, Majesty. They are in league with sense,
               Order and even silence. They are in the pay
               Of thought and of communication.

LEADER: Then they have betrayed their sacred trust
               For theirs is a mission of division and destruction.

CAPTAIN: Our first witness will explain the functions of language.

PROFESSOR: History is a dialogue
               Between forward and backward
               Going inevitably forward by the abuse of thought
               And the gradual destruction of intelligence.
               Now the function of the word is
               To designate: first the machine,
               Then what the machine produces,
               And finally what the machine destroys.
               Words have no other function.
               They belong by right to the political process:
               Doing, making, destroying. Or rather
               Being done, being made, being destroyed.
               Such is history.

CAPTAIN: This witness can prove that language is the enemy of
               history and should therefore be abolished.

LEADER: Let him proceed.

PROFESSOR: The word is a means of locomotion
               Forward and backward
               Along the infinite horizontal plane
               Created by the history
               Which words themselves destroy

(Substituting what *ought* to have happened
For what actually happened).

LEADER: But if that is the case, Language is the fulfilment of
history. Why then should it be destroyed?

PROFESSOR: The machine must always destroy
The maker of the machine, for this proves
That the machine is greater than the one who made it
Just as man is more important than God.
Words reflect this principle, in their relation to history.
Words create history. But they, in turn,
Must be destroyed by the history they have created.
The word supersedes the event, as light emerges from
darkness,
Transforming the event into something it was not.
But the event, in turn, supersedes its interpretation as
darkness
Replaces light, and in the end it is darkness that wins.
And the Words of the historian are forgotten.

LEADER: Which then is real? The light, or the darkness?

PROFESSOR: Words create reality as fast as they are eaten by it,
And they destroy reality as fast as they themselves
Come back to life, out of the minds of men.
This is the movement of history:
The backward, forward working of the web;
The plunge forward, into the web,
The struggle backward, but not out of the web.

LEADER: Words, then, are the ultimate reality! Let there never
again be any silence. Let tongues never be still. For if
there be silence, our history will instantly be unmade,
and if we stop talking we will cease to exist. Words,

therefore, are acquitted. Let Silence be called to the stand.

CAPTAIN: One moment! It is not so simple. There are three kinds of language. There is true language, there is falsehood, and there is propaganda. Let us call all three to the stand, beginning with the most dangerous.

LEADER: Call Truth to the stand!

CLERK: Truth, tell us your name.

TRUTH: My name is Truth.

CLERK: Where do you live?

TRUTH: In things as they are, in minds that see things as they are, in wills that conform to things as they are.

LAWYER: Truth, you are the enemy of the Mammoth State.
You have pretended to serve us, and you have
All the while poisoned the minds of the people
With enemy doctrines. You refuse
To conform your declarations to the pure
Slogans of our Leader. You are therefore
Insubordinate, a saboteur, a spy,
A tool of the enemy.
How many murders, bombings, acts
Of open or hidden violence have you
Not committed against us? You are
The worst of enemies. You are
The destroyer of the Tower.

VOICES: To the salt mines! To the salt mines!

TRUTH: You are your own enemies. You destroyed your own Tower.

VOICES: Put him to death.
Shoot him! Down with him!
Kill him. He is the People's enemy.

SECOND PHILOSOPHER: I can defend Truth.

CAPTAIN: Shall we hear this witness?

LEADER: Give him one minute, not more.

SECOND PHILOSOPHER: There is no need to put Truth to death.
Truth has never existed, there is no Truth.
Everything is vague. The world, O Leader,
Which only seems to exist,
Needs to be expressed in words which seem to exist.
Actually, nothing has real being.
Seeming is existing. Everything that seems,
Is. It is what it wants to be.
It has no being, only wanting.
Truth, then, may seem to exist.
But what is it? If we look too close
We see right through the seeming.
Leader, there is no Truth.

VOICES: He is right! There is no truth!

OTHER VOICES: He is a liar! Truth exists, but it is not true.

LEADER: Truth or no Truth, words are agents of the traitor:
Meaning. Let them be put to death.

VOICES: Death, death, death,
Let words be put to death!

CAPTAIN: One moment!
Not all words claim to be true.
The pure, holy, divine words of the Leader,
What are they? Are they true?
[*Awkward silence, broken by the* LEADER.]

LEADER: Send this witness to the salt mines.
I have words of my own. Call Propaganda to the stand!

CLERK: Do you swear to conceal the truth, the whole truth
and to confuse nothing but the issue?

PROPAGANDA: I do.

LEADER: What is your name?

PROPAGANDA: Legion.

LEADER: Where do you live?

PROPAGANDA: In the heads of the people.

LEADER: What do the people look like?

PROPAGANDA: Zombies.

LEADER: How long have they looked like zombies?

PROPAGANDA: Since we got inside.

LEADER: How did you get inside?

PROPAGANDA: By shots in the arm, by beatings over the head, noises in the ear and all the right kind of medicines.

LEADER: Who destroyed the Tower?

PROPAGANDA: The religious warmongers, the clergy, the freemasons, the Pope, the millionaires, the Elders of Zion, the Young Men's Christian Association, the Jesuits and the Legion of Mary.

LEADER: You are a faithful guardian of the Mammoth Democracy, you shall be decorated with the order of the Tower and you shall possess exclusive freedom of speech and worship in every part of the world. Go forth and form the minds of the young. [*Turning to* CLERK] Call Falsehood to the stand.

[*Solemn music—enter* FALSEHOOD.]

VOICE: This must be one of the gods.

LEADER: Sir, who are you?

FALSEHOOD: Why, I am Truth.

LEADER: Ah, yes. We should have known.

FALSEHOOD: I built the Tower.

VOICES: The builder of the Tower, the builder of the Tower!

LEADER: Your worship, will you be so kind as to tell us the function of language, and indicate whether or not words had anything to do with the ruin of the tower? Are words faithful to our cause, or should they be done away with? Can our empire subsist without language?

FALSEHOOD: I am your strength. Without me you fall. I will give you the only words that will serve your purpose. You should never have listened to anyone but me. Your city is made in my image and likeness. I penetrate reality by destroying it. Those who follow me will be split in half and each one, instead of being one man, will become two angels. If you follow me and listen to my words, you will find this out for yourself.

CAPTAIN: This must be the voice of our creator.

LEADER: Tell us, Majesty, who destroyed the Tower?

FALSEHOOD: The Tower has never been destroyed. Just as I am immortal, the Tower is indestructible. The Tower is a spiritual reality and so am I. The Tower is everywhere. What you call the fall of the Tower was only its beginning, its passage into a new, more active phase of existence. The Tower is not a building but an influence, a mentality, an invisible power. The Tower stands, and I am the King who lives on the summit of the Tower. And because I am everywhere, everywhere is the Tower of Babel.

LEADER: Divine and omnipresent Majesty, forgive us for not having recognized you. What shall we do with the people who resist your authority?

FALSEHOOD: Let all men serve me in chains.

CHORUS: Grow, Babylon, grow,
Serve your Lord in chains.
Chains will be your liberty.

Grow, Babylon, grow!

CLERK: There is one more witness!

LEADER: Who is he?

CAPTAIN: His name is Silence.

LEADER: Useless! Throw him out! Let silence be crucified!

[*Music, an all-out crucifixion of silence.*]

PART TWO—The City of God

Scene One—Zodiac

[SCENE—*A river bank.*]

RAPHAEL, THOMAS, PROPHET, CHILDREN

RAPHAEL: Once there was a city where these marshes are,
                    Ships at dockside, barrels on the quay,
                    Children running between the wheels
                    Watching the foreigner's sandal
                    Fearing the unknown words of the men with scars.

THOMAS: Now all is sand, and grass, and water
                    Where the rank marsh draws down one crooked gull.
                    Men have gone from this place. There is
                    Neither cursing, nor praying, nor dancing.
                    Neither living nor dying, buying nor selling.
                    No more traffic on the water front
                    No more pianos in the cabaret.

PROPHET: The city under the sand
                    Lives everywhere. It is not a buried city.
                    The westward ships will soon discover
                    The old city, on another continent
                    Young and new. The southward ships
                    Will find that the city was never destroyed.
                    The northward plane soon sees the sun
                    Shine on the towers of the same Babylon.

RAPHAEL: The stars pursue their prey.
                    Across the edge of the sky
                    Time moves east and west

Covering the land with light and darkness,
Life and death, truth and illusion.
The hills stand where they were before,
The stars pass by.

CHILDREN: Washed in winter's rivers
Ancient seasons come:
Cancer and Orion,
The Bear and Capricorn.

PROPHET: Men were made to be the mirror of God. They were meant to be one mirror filled with His one light. When will the pieces be brought together again, and receive the divine image?

CHILDREN: Washed in silent streams
The Lion and the Twins
Come crowned in diadems
With weapons in their hands.

RAPHAEL: Words once contained the silences beyond the stars. Words given us by God, bound minds in agreement, and in agreement made them strong. Because they were strong, men became free. They were free because they thought the same thing. They were strong because they knew the same truth and lived by it, working together.

CHILDREN: The Beast stands in the sky
With poison in his thorn.
The Archer bides his time
And death hangs on his arm.

PROPHET: But the languages of men have become empty palaces
Where the winds blow in every room.
Strange spirits sing in them. The ruined houses are
Hiding-places for men at arms.

CHILDREN: Washed in splendid rain
            The Bull, the fishes come,
            The Crab, the Waterman,
            And put their packages down.

PROPHET: The Word of God, coming from afar,
            Is always near: Near in the stillness of the thing that
                moves,
            Near in the silence of the thing that speaks.
            Near, not dead, even in the heart of one that lies.
            His silence is always near. His Word is near.
            We cannot listen. We turn away fearing an accuser.

CHILDREN: Washed in silent peace
            The Swan and Sirius come,
            The Virgin with the Scales,
            The wind, and the bone moon.

PROPHET: In the last days the Word, wise without omen, strong
            without armies, will come to the crossroads of the
            broken universe. Then Truth will speak to the dead.
            Then God will awaken them from oblivion with His
            Word, and they shall sit up in their tombs, and look
            upon the Word Whom they have slain, and recognize
            His eyes like wine.

CHILDREN: Storms and tides of spring
            Divide their chains and come.
            The ram rides in their brine
            Stronger than the sun.

PROPHET: Do not think the destroyed city is entirely evil. As a
            symbol is destroyed to give place to a reality, so the
            shadow of Babylon will be destroyed to give place to
            the light which it might have contained. Men will
            indeed be of one tongue, and they will indeed build

a city that will reach from earth to heaven. This new city will not be the tower of sin, but the City of God. Not the wisdom of men shall build this city, nor their machines, not their power. But the great city shall be built without hands, without labor, without money and without plans. It will be a perfect city, built on eternal foundations, and it shall stand forever, because it is built by the thought and the silence and the wisdom and the power of God. But you, my brothers, and I are stones in the wall of this city. Let us run to find our places. Though we may run in the dark, our destiny is full of glory.

THE ANCIENT, PROPHET, RAPHAEL, THOMAS, DANCERS, FIRST VILLAGER, SECOND VILLAGER, EXILES, CHORUS

[SCENE—*A village on a river.*]

THE ANCIENT: By the ever changing waters
      We sit down and weep
      As if we had some other home.

CHORUS: Lord, when the skies fall down to hell
      Who will stop the giant wheel
      Who will break the strict machine
      Who will save us from the mill?

RAPHAEL: Exiles, where have you come from,
      Where are you going?

CHORUS: We found no man to lead us into our own land
      Because we found no man to tell us of our own land.
      We have forgotten where we came from. How can
       we tell
      Where we might be going?

THE ANCIENT: As long as I can remember we have wandered by
       these rivers
      We have wept by these waters
      As if we had some other home.

CHORUS: Who will define movement and rest,
      Who will distinguish strength and fear,
      Give us a name that tells the mind
      More than an echo in the ear?

THE ANCIENT: I have heard my Fathers say that we came from an-
       other country.

FIRST EXILE: One by one we lost our names.
Men gave us numbers.

SECOND EXILE: Words were poured over us like water.
Sentences ran down our necks
Like sand. Sand and water,
Good and evil, truth and lies
All were the same.

FIRST EXILE: There are no actions
Only explanations.
Men give us numbers.

THE ANCIENT: For years there has been found
No man to teach us.

SECOND EXILE: No word to wash our wounded minds.

FIRST EXILE: The words of this land
Are interminable signals of their own emptiness,
Signs without meaning.

SECOND EXILE: Our speeches have ended in exhaustion.

CHORUS: Lord, when the pieces of the world
Melt in the enfolding flame
Who will raise our bones from death,
Who will call us back again?
How shall we hear and understand
A word that we have never learned
A name that we were never told
A cry that man has never made?

PROPHET: If you have not heard your name, it is not because
it has not been spoken. The Lord, Who names you,
lives within you. You live by the name he utters in
secret. This is the hope that you are rooted in.

FIRST EXILE: Is there then hope within us?

SECOND EXILE: Are we rooted in something?

PROPHET: If you exist, you exist in hope. To cease hoping is to cease existing. To hope, and to exist, is to have roots in God. But one can hope and yet be hopeless: that is, one can exist without believing in one's existence. The man who does not believe in his own existence is rooted in despair. But he could not despair if he were not able to hope. Your existence, though you despair, is rooted in hope.

FIRST EXILE: Why must we despair?

SECOND EXILE: Why must we live in fear,
As if our life were cursed by stars,
As if the wheel of the sky would, without fail,
Drag us to a bad end?

RAPHAEL: Stars are too wise to think of you,
Too innocent to harm you.

THOMAS: They are the signals of the Christ,
Who holds them in His hand.

THOMAS: You will wait for their light in winter
Learning discipline.
You will work until they come in summertime
When the words of God will be planted among you,
Growing in work and patience.

FIRST EXILE: Is there work for us, somewhere, without slavery?

SECOND EXILE: Is there a discipline that will give us peace?

PROPHET: Christ's mercy heals the regions of the mind.
Blessed by Him our acts are free.
Heard by Him
Our silences bear fruit. All our words become true.

THE ANCIENT: Ah, yes, I have heard in the past that words could be true.

RAPHAEL: They are meant to bind minds together in the joy
of truth.

THOMAS: You must discover new words reborn out of an old
time
Like new seeds from an old harvest
If you would bless the world with rest and labor,
With speech and silence
And crown your peace with timeless blossoms
When the strong Child climbs quietly to His throne.

THE ANCIENT: Our Fathers told us that before we were made cap-
tives we lived in our own villages and worked the
land, worshipped together, held festivals. There were
marriages. There were harvests. Children were born
and the old people were laid to rest in the Church's
shadow. Men spoke to one another quietly in the
market place, and one man could agree with another.

RAPHAEL: Villages are slow to forget
The silences of ancient years.
Houses and churches cling together
Fastened by the words of older generations
And by the silences of the dead Fathers.
So windows stare together at the sun.
Smokes of separate houses
Climb the morning sky together.
Meals are made together.
The same swallows twitter together
Under the shutters of the houses.
One clear bell tells all times,
One same small bell
Recalls the silence of the blessed Fathers.

THE ANCIENT: Look, here is a village! Here is a festival!

FIRST EXILE: Houses see their faces in the water,
Dressed in flags and vines. Boats and wagons
Gather. Flowering wagons and crowned oxen!

SECOND EXILE: There are blue and yellow canopies
For flute, fiddle and drum.

RAPHAEL: Singing together, dancing together
Signify that the people are one.

DANCERS: Once a body had a soul
They were in agreement.
Said the body to the soul,
I will be your raiment.
Said the spirit to the flesh
Now we are a person.

RAPHAEL: When hills are dressed in vines and fruit
And houses see their faces in the water,
They send their boats into the noonday sun.

FIRST VILLAGER: Music and dancing signify
That we are one.
So we laugh in the decorated square,
Dancing around the fiddlers under the awning.

SECOND VILLAGER: Those who sing in the boats, trailing their fingers
in the water, echo the dancers on the shore.

DANCERS: Once a person had a friend
They were in agreement.
Said the person to his friend,
Take my heart and keep it.
You and I will live alike
As a single person.

THOMAS: Look, there are two villages. One, on the shore, is
the real village. The other, upside down in the
water, is the image of the first. The houses of the

real village are solid, the houses in the water are destroyed by the movements in the water, but re-create their image in the stillness that follows.

RAPHAEL: So it is with our world. The city of men, on earth, is the inverted reflection of another city. What is eternal and unchanging stands reflected in the restless waters of time, and many of the events of our history are simply movements in the water that destroy the temporal shadow of eternity. We who are obsessed with movement, measure the importance of events by their power to unsettle our world. We look for meaning only in the cataclysms which obscure the image of reality. But all the things pass away, and the picture of the real city returns, although there may be no one left to recognize it, or to understand.

FIRST VILLAGER: In the gray hours before dawn
When horses stir in the stable,
Swallows twitter outside the shutter,
The streets smell of fresh bread,
And when the churchdoor opens
One can see the lighted candles in the shadows,
And listen to the sacring bell.

SECOND VILLAGER: Before the sun was up
We had already milked the cows,
Watered the horses, hitched up the teams.
We worked together in one another's fields,
Bringing home the hay.
Everybody's grapes will redden the gutters
When we make wine together, in September.

FIRST VILLAGER: And now we all unite

To celebrate a wedding. In this festival
We dance together because we are glad
To be living together. We have heard
The same songs before, at other weddings.
That is why we play them now.
We find ourselves made new
In singing what was sung before.

DANCERS: Once a person had a friend
They were in agreement.
Said the person to his friend
Take my heart and keep it.
You and I will live alike
As a single person.

THE ANCIENT: These people do not sit together by the waters and weep, as we are accustomed to. Why is it that they are happy, while we have always lived in sorrow?

PROPHET: These are the men who have never been conquered by the builders of the ancient tower. Because they do not kill with the sword, they do not fear death. Because they do not live by the machine, they fear no insecurity. Since they say what they mean, they are able to love another, and since they live mostly in silence they know what is the beginning of life, and its meaning and its end. For they are the children of God.

THE ANCIENT: How is it that the whole world is not like this?

RAPHAEL: It shall be so, for Babylon has fallen.
[*Sound of a distant trumpet.*]

THOMAS: Listen, I hear a trumpet
From beyond the hills.

RAPHAEL: It announces the great messenger.

VOICE [*slowly, out of the distance*]: "I will destroy the name of Babylon, and the remains, and the bud, and the offspring, saith the Lord."

THOMAS: Whose voice was that?

RAPHAEL: *Dicit Leo—*

It was the Lion of Isaias,
Waking on the watchtower.
The desert-thrasher,
Seeing beyond mountains,
Whole nights upon his tower.

CHORUS: It was the Lion
Who sees in the dark
Who hunts upon the mountains:
By whom the enemy lies killed.

[*Trumpets. Sounds of a storm and of a distant battle.*]

PROPHET: Now is the time when the great city must at last fall
By the power of its own curse. Cursed by God
Because its builders cursed themselves,
They hated peace, refused the blessing.
They hated to be themselves, hated to be men.
Wanting to be gods, they were made less than themselves.
They might have become gods
If they had deigned to remain men.

CHORUS: In one hour, O Babylon,
In one night hour, after so many years,
After so much blood, and so much power,
In one small hour you lie destroyed.

RAPHAEL: Yours was a long hot day that burned the earth,
and now

Your sun goes down in fire and rain
Not without glory. But it is not your glory,
Babylon: destroyed in one hour,
You shall be forgotten forever.

VOICE   [*out of the distance*]: Babylon the great is fallen, is
fallen
And is become the house of emptiness
And is carried away by the night birds.
The kings have seen her, drowning in the sea.

CHORUS: Fire can quench water
Flame can stand upon foam
Blood lies on the rock
When the sea goes home.
Nails can give back thunder
Fire can leap from wood
And mercy from the Heart of Man
Though that Heart be dead.

[RAPHAEL *and* THOMAS *speak against the background of the* CHORUS.]

THOMAS: I hear the voices of the islands. What do they sing?
RAPHAEL: They sing that Babylon has fallen.
THOMAS: I hear the voices of the hills. What do they sing?
RAPHAEL: They say there shall be no more war.
THOMAS: I hear the voices of the Cities. What do they sing?
RAPHAEL: There is no more despair!

CHORUS: We know the Word of God is spoken
Never to be forgotten.
Not to be echoed in the ear,
Printed upon a piece of paper
And forgotten.

THOMAS: How was Babylon destroyed?

CHORUS: By one Word uttered in silence
Babylon is destroyed.

THOMAS: But by what one word was Babylon destroyed?

RAPHAEL: By the One Word Who is in the beginning, and Who
sustains all things, and Who shall be in the end.
He was, and He is, and He shall be. He Who Is has
only to be mentioned, and all He knows not is no
longer known.

THOMAS: Who is the Word, the Beginning and the End?

RAPHAEL: He is the King of Glory!

CHORUS: *In Principio.*

PROPHET: The Word of God on high
Is the fountain of wisdom.
His ways are eternal commandments.

CHORUS: *Erat Verbum.*
Et Verbum erat apud Deum

PROPHET: The Word leaped down in darkness men could touch
Nor did the dark deliver them.

CHORUS: *Et Deus erat Verbum.*

RAPHAEL: The Word held open the divided sea
Until the tide drowned kings.
The Word spoke on the Mountain.

CHORUS: *Et Deus erat Verbum.*

PROPHET: Men who were bitten in the desert
Grew well, remembering the Word
Or seeing His mysterious sign.

CHORUS: *Verbum caro factum,*
Verbum sanctum!

THOMAS: Flesh did not understand
The Word made flesh.

Those who feared the voice of thunder
Scorned to eat the Word made Bread.

CHORUS: *Verbum crucis,*
Verbum sanctum.

THOMAS: Not wheat, nor meat
Nor meal, nor bread:
The Word was given in the desert
Where snow endured the force of fire.
The Word came down upon the wilderness
Touching the tongues of men in crystal morsels.

CHORUS: *Verbum crucis,*
Verbum pacis.

PROPHET: Those who have taken peace upon their tongue
Have eaten heaven:
They have made heaven in the midst of us,
Jerusalem in Babylon.

CHORUS: *Verbum crucis.*

RAPHAEL: This is the Word the prophet saw:
This is the tender plant
The bleeding root in his despised report:
The Word who would not speak when He was
wounded.

CHORUS: *Verbum sanctum.*

PROPHET: Give rest, give rest, O Lord,
To the slain souls who sing beneath the altar.
Give the robes and rest and thrones to the white
martyrs
Who swore and signed with their own blood:
"Thy words are true!"

CHORUS: *Adorate verbum sanctum in aeternum.*

ALL: Lo the Word and the white horse

With eyes of flame to judge and fight
Power and meekness in His hand
Mercy in His look like wine.
He alone can break the seal
And tell the conquerors His Name.

ADORATE DOMINUM!

PART THREE

BIRDCAGE WALK

1

One royal afternoon
When I was young and easily surprised
By uncles coming from the park
At the command of nurses and of guards,

I wondered, over trees and ponds,
At the sorry, rude walls
And the white windows of the apartments.

"These," said my uncle, "are the tallest houses."

2

Yes, in the spring of my joy
When I was visibly affected by a gaitered bishop,
Large and unsteady in the flagged yard,
Guards, dogs and blackbirds fled on every hand.

"He is an old one," said uncle,
"The gaiters are real."

3

Rippled, fistfed windows of your
Dun high houses! Then
Come cages made of pretty willows
Where they put the palace girls!
Green ducks wade slowly from the marble water.
One swan reproves a saucy daughter.

I consider my own true pond,
Look for the beginning and the end.
I lead the bishop down lanes and islands.

4

Yes, in the windows of my first existence
Before my yawns became seasons,
When nurses and uncles were sure,
Chinese fowl fought the frosty water
Startled by this old pontifex.

"No bridge" (He smiled
Between the budding branches),
"No crossing to the cage
Of the paradise bird!"

Astounded by the sermons in the leaves
I cried, "No! No! The stars have higher houses!"

Kicking the robins and ganders
From the floor of his insular world
The magic bishop leaned his blessing on the children.

5

That was the bold day when
Moved by the unexpected summons
I opened all the palace aviaries
As by a king's representative
I was appointed fowler.

LANDSCAPE

1

A Personage is seen
Leaning upon a cushion
Printed with cornflowers.

A Child appears
Holding up a pencil.

"This is a picture
(Says the Child to the Personage)
Of the vortex."

"Draw it your own way,"
Says the Personage.

(Music is heard
Pure in the island windows,
Sea-music on the Child's
Interminable shore, his coral home.)

Behind a blue mountain
Covered with chickenfoot trees,
The molten sun appears,
A heavy, painted flower.

A Personage is seen
Leaning upon the mountain
With the sun in one hand
And a pencil in the other.

"This is a picture
(Says the Personage to the Child)
Of the beginning of the world."

"Or of its end!" cries the Child
Hiding himself in the cushions.

2

A Woman appears
Leaning upon the Child's shoulder.
He looks up again.

"This is my Mother
(Says the Child to the Personage)
Older than the moon."

(Grecian horses are heard
Returning from the foam
Of the pure island's windows,
And the Child's horizons.)

"My Mother is a world
(Says the Child to the Personage)
Printed with gillyflowers."

"Paint her your own way"
(Says the Personage to the Child).
And, lifting up his pencil,
He crosses out the sun.

WISDOM

I studied it and it taught me nothing.
I learned it and soon forgot everything else:
Having forgotten, I was burdened with knowledge—
The insupportable knowledge of nothing.

How sweet my life would be, if I were wise!
Wisdom is well known
When it is no longer seen or thought of.
Only then is understanding bearable.

"WHEN IN THE SOUL OF THE SERENE DISCIPLE . . ."

When in the soul of the serene disciple
With no more Fathers to imitate
Poverty is a success,
It is a small thing to say the roof is gone:
He has not even a house.

Stars, as well as friends,
Are angry with the noble ruin.
Saints depart in several directions.

Be still:
There is no longer any need of comment.
It was a lucky wind
That blew away his halo with his cares,
A lucky sea that drowned his reputation.

Here you will find
Neither a proverb nor a memorandum.
There are no ways,
No methods to admire
Where poverty is no achievement.
His God lives in his emptiness like an affliction.

What choice remains?
Well, to be ordinary is not a choice:
It is the usual freedom
Of men without visions.

IN SILENCE

Be still
Listen to the stones of the wall.
Be silent, they try
To speak your

Name.
Listen
To the living walls.
Who are you?
Who
Are you? Whose
Silence are you?

Who (be quiet)
Are you (as these stones
Are quiet). Do not
Think of what you are
Still less of
What you may one day be.
Rather
Be what you are (but who?) be
The unthinkable one
You do not know.

O be still, while
You are still alive,
And all things live around you
Speaking (I do not hear)

To your own being,
Speaking by the Unknown
That is in you and in themselves.

"I will try, like them
To be my own silence:
And this is difficult. The whole
World is secretly on fire. The stones
Burn, even the stones
They burn me. How can a man be still or
Listen to all things burning? How can he dare
To sit with them when
All their silence
Is on fire?"

EARLY MASS

(St Joseph Infirmary—Louisville)

There is a Bread which You and I propose.
It is Your truth. And more: it is ourselves.
There was a wickedness whose end is blessing.
Come, people, to the Cross and Wedding!

His are the mysteries which I expound
And mine the children whom His stars befriend.
Our Christ has cleanly built His sacred town.

What do the windows of His city say?
His innocence is written on your sky!
Because we think His Latin we are part of one another,
Together when I am away.

Come to the ark and stone
Come to the Holies where His work is done,
Dear hasty doves, transparent in His sun!

Gather us God in honeycombs,
My Israel, in the Ohio valley!
For brightness falls upon our dark.

Death owns a wasted kingdom.
Bless and restore the blind, straighten the broken limb.
These mended stones shall build Jerusalem.

Come to the golden fence with folded hands
And see your Bird, kneel to your white Beloved.
Here is your Father at my finger's end!

The clouds are torn. Summon the winds of fall.
On street and water, track and river, shine, November!
Open the doors and own the avenue
For see: we are the makers of a risen world,
    the brothers of a new
Brown universe whose liturgy
Sweetly consumes my bones.

A PRELUDE: FOR THE FEAST OF ST. AGNES

O small St. Agnes, dressed in gold
With fire and rainbows round about your face:
Sing with the martyrs in my Mass's Canon!

Come home, come home, old centuries
Whose soundless islands ring me from within,
Whose saints walk down a winter morning's iris,
Wait upon this altar stone
(Some of them holding palms
But others hyacinths!).

I speak your name with wine upon my lips
Drowned in the singing of the quiet catacomb.
My feet upon forget-me-nots
I sink this little frigate in the Blood of silence
And put my pall upon the cup
Working the mystery of peace, whose mercies must
Run down and find us, Saint, by Saint John's stairs.

No lines, no globes,
No compasses, no staring fires
No candle's cup to swing upon
My night's dark ocean.

There the pretended horns of time grow dim.
No tunes, no signals claim us any more.
The cities cry, perhaps, like peacocks.
But the cloud has come.

I kneel in this stone corner having blood upon my wrist
And blood upon my breast,
O small St. Agnes, dressed in martyrdom
With fire and water waving in your hair.

THE ANNUNCIATION

Ashes of paper, ashes of a world
Wandering, when fire is done:
We argue with the drops of rain!

Until One comes Who walks unseen
Even in elements we have destroyed.
Deeper than any nerve
He enters flesh and bone.
Planting His truth, He puts our substance on.
Air, earth and rain
Rework the frame that fire has ruined.
What was dead is waiting for His Flame.
Sparks of His Spirit spend their seeds, and hide
To grow like irises, born before summertime.
These blue things bud in Israel.

The girl prays by the bare wall
Between the lamp and the chair.
(Framed with an angel in our galleries
She has a richer painted room, sometimes a crown.
Yet seven pillars of obscurity
Build her to Wisdom's house, and Ark, and Tower.
She is the Secret of another Testament
She owns their manna in her jar.)

Fifteen years old—
The flowers printed on her dress
Cease moving in the middle of her prayer

When God, Who sends the messenger,
Meets His messenger in her Heart.
Her answer, between breath and breath,
Wrings from her innocence our Sacrament!
In her white body God becomes our Bread.

It is her tenderness
Heats the dead world like David on his bed.
Times that were too soon criminal
And never wanted to be normal
Evade the beast that has pursued
You, me and Adam out of Eden's wood.
Suddenly we find ourselves assembled
Cured and recollected under several green trees.

Her prudence wrestled with the Dove
To hide us in His cloud of steel and silver:
These are the mysteries of her Son.
And here my heart, a purchased outlaw,
Prays in her possession
Until her Jesus makes my heart
Smile like a flower in her blameless hand.

SINCERITY

Omnis homo mendax

As for the liar, fear him less
Than one who thinks himself sincere,
Who, having deceived himself,
Can deceive you with a good conscience.

One who doubts his own truth
May mistrust another less:

Knowing in his own heart,
That all men are liars
He will be less outraged
When he is deceived by another.

So, too, will he sooner believe
In the sincerity of God.

The sincerity of God! Who never justifies
His actions to men! Who makes no bargains
With any other sincerity, because He knows
There is no other! Who does what He pleases
And never protests His innocence!

Which of us can stand the sincerity of God?

Which of us can bear a Lord
Who is neither guilty nor innocent
(Who cannot be innocent because He cannot be guilty)?

What has our sincerity to do with His
Whose truth is no approval of our truth
And is not judged by anyone,
Even by Himself?

(Yet if I think myself sincere
I will approve the purity of God
Convinced that my own purity
Is approved by Him.)

So, when the Lord speaks, we go to sleep
Or turn quickly to some more congenial business
Since, as every liar knows,
No man can bear such sincerity.

TO A SEVERE NUN

I know, Sister, that solitude
Will never dismay you. You have chosen
A path too steep for others to follow.
I take it you prefer to go without them.

You will not complain that others are fickle
When they abandon you, renouncing the contest.
After all, they have not understood
That love is a contest, and that the love you demand
Is a match, in which you overcome your friends
After a long agony.

Thus you have no visible companions. Yet, drive on,
Drive on: do not consider your despair! Imagine rather
That there are many saints around you in the same desperation,
Violent, without contact, without responsibility,
Except of course to their own just souls
And to the God Who cannot blame them.

You know where you are going. You alone
In the whole convent know what bitter comfort
Eludes the malcontents who travel this unusual desert,
Seeking the impossible, and not the Absolute—
Sustained always by the same hate.

Do not be disconcerted, Sister, if in spite of your effort
The impertinent truth shows up weakness at least in others
And distracts you with their suffering.

Do not be humbled if, for an instant,
Christ seems glad to suffer in another.

Forget this scandal. Do not look at them
Or you may lose your nerve, and come to admit
That violence is your evasion and that you,
You most of all, are weak.

ELEGY FOR THE MONASTERY BARN

As though an aged person were to wear
Too gay a dress
And walk about the neighborhood
Announcing the hour of her death,

So now, one summer day's end,
At suppertime, when wheels are still,
The long barn suddenly puts on the traitor, beauty,
And hails us with a dangerous cry,
For: "Look!" she calls to the country,
"Look how fast I dress myself in fire!"

Had we half guessed how long her spacious shadows
Harbored a woman's vanity
We would be less surprised to see her now
So loved, and so attended, and so feared.

She, in whose airless heart
We burst our veins to fill her full of hay,
Now stands apart.
She will not have us near her. Terribly,
Sweet Christ, how terribly her beauty burns us now!

And yet she has another legacy,
More delicate, to leave us, and more rare.

Who knew her solitude?
Who heard the peace downstairs

While flames ran whispering among the rafters?
Who felt the silence, there,
The long, hushed gallery
Clean and resigned and waiting for the fire?

Look! They have all come back to speak their summary:
Fifty invisible cattle, the past years
Assume their solemn places one by one.
This is the little minute of their destiny.
Here is their meaning found. Here is their end.

Laved in the flame as in a Sacrament
The brilliant walls are holy
In their first-last hour of joy.

Fly from within the barn! Fly from the silence
Of this creature sanctified by fire!
Let no man stay inside to look upon the Lord!
Let no man wait within and see the Holy
One sitting in the presence of disaster
Thinking upon this barn His gentle doom!

STRANGER

When no one listens
To the quiet trees
When no one notices
The sun in the pool

Where no one feels
The first drop of rain
Or sees the last star

Or hails the first morning
Of a giant world
Where peace begins
And rages end:

One bird sits still
Watching the work of God:
One turning leaf,
Two falling blossoms,
Ten circles upon the pond.

One cloud upon the hillside,
Two shadows in the valley
And the light strikes home.
Now dawn commands the capture
Of the tallest fortune,
The surrender
Of no less marvelous prize!

Closer and clearer
Than any wordy master,

Thou inward Stranger
Whom I have never seen,

Deeper and cleaner
Than the clamorous ocean,
Seize up my silence
Hold me in Thy Hand!

Now act is waste
And suffering undone
Laws become prodigals
Limits are torn down
For envy has no property
And passion is none.

Look, the vast Light stands still
Our cleanest Light is One!